Smile, Smile, Smile!

Poems
by

GURUMAYI
CHIDVILASANANDA

CSP

A SIDDHA YOGA MEDITATION PUBLICATION
PUBLISHED BY CHITSHAKTI PUBLICATIONS, CHENNAI

ACKNOWLEDGMENTS

With enormous gratitude, on behalf of seekers of the Truth now and for generations to come, we thank Gurumayi for sharing her beautiful inner song, inviting us all on this pilgrimage to the Great Lord.

Editor

First published in 1998 by SYDA Foundation® New York, USA.

First published in India in 1999 by Chitshakti Publications, Chennai.

Printed by Usha Multigraphs, Pvt. Ltd., Mumbai.

FOR SALE ONLY IN INDIA, SRI LANKA, NEPAL AND BHUTAN.

ISBN: 81-86693-15-7

Contents

CONTENTS

CONTENTS

The touch of your smile will make
every facet of your destiny shimmer
like the colours of the rainbow.

Introduction

THE THIRTY-ONE POEMS in *Smile, Smile, Smile!* provide a rare glimpse into the mind and heart of a remarkable being, the Siddha Master Gurumayi Chidvilasananda. The poems are improvisations by Gurumayi on the New Year's talk she delivered at the beginning of 1998, "Refresh your resolution. Smile at your destiny." Gurumayi combines in these verses an often playful tone with teachings of the utmost seriousness. Selecting phrases and ideas from her New Year's talk, she embroiders upon them in the most unpredictable, delightful and penetrating ways.

In the following stanza, for instance, Gurumayi proffers a glimpse of the true nature of time:

> When I become aware of Time,
>   an extraordinary sense of freedom
>   rushes through my spirit.

I am given the wondrous opportunity
    to live life fully again and again.
The kindness of Time grants me
    a million exhilarating reasons
    to rejoice and let my heart sing
    the Guru's sacred name.

So many people regard time as a prison and destiny as sealed. A *siddha* sees time from an exalted perspective, in which life opens out anew moment by moment.

While letting her heart sing through these poems, Gurumayi crafts explicit aphorisms and embeds subtle hints that illuminate the challenges of living a spiritual life. At the same time, she demonstrates the actual process of spiritual contemplation, modelling the ways to use a text like the New Year's talk as a beacon to shine into every nook and cranny of our lives. For example, during the talk, which appears in print for the first time in this book, she quotes a statement from the *Vedas* that begins, "When God smiles . . ." Starting from that phrase, Gurumayi writes a poem that opens with these powerful lines:

When God smiles,
    the force of all forces,
    the *sahasrāra*, throbs.
The effect of the sound
    showers nectar.

The light of all lights
    infuses the field of the body,
    which responds with exultation.

The strength of these poems is such that I find it hard to read more than one or two at a sitting. A poem will sink into me and then go off like a depth charge, exploding habitual notions and throwing me open to deeper awareness. In one of her poems Gurumayi shows how a deepening awareness allows us to penetrate the mind and ultimately to transform our lives. In a section near the beginning of "The Light of Your Awareness" she explains:

When you lose an object in the dark,
    you can find it with a candle
    or a flashlight. You can turn on a lamp.
But when you lose your thoughts,
    ideas, intentions and goals
    in the dark field of your mind,
    how will you regain them?
Only the light of your awareness
    can illumine the field of your mind.

Why does it seem so natural for these illuminating improvisations by Gurumayi to take the form of poetry? Probably because poetry is the oldest and most universal form for communicating things that matter. For a spiritual Master, in particular, such spontaneous poetry seems like an outburst of her irrepressible ecstasy, creativity and playfulness. Over the ages, many great saints and spiritual masters have cast their teachings in poetry for the delectation and illumination of their students. The Sufi saint Rumi, for instance, uttered thousands of lines of verse extemporaneously, which were taken down for posterity by one of his close disciples. In this book, Gurumayi picks up the pen and graciously offers her outpourings directly to us.

Her poems emanate from the pure space of the heart, a space that is touchingly intimate. When I read them, I have the uncanny sense of being in the room with Gurumayi, listening as she responds directly to questions and requests from a lively gathering of seekers. "What is it like to have a steadfast mind?" "How do I set off in a new direction?" "Please, speak about the nature of the Goddess." It's almost as if the verse lines of her responses are a "voiceprint" of the workings of this *siddha's* resplendent mind, exposing the silky texture of what it feels like to know oneself completely and to offer one's life unreservedly in service.

Exploring in detail in these poems what she means by resolution and destiny (and also what she means by refreshing and smiling), Gurumayi extracts abundant teachings that can spark the most profound contemplation. These poems illustrate, too, the very process of distilling teachings from a spiritual text. Each of us, in fact, might choose phrases or themes from the New Year's talk and write down responses — whether in poetry or in prose — in order to evoke our own ways of refreshing resolution and smiling at destiny.

The difference between prose and poetry is like the difference between walking and dancing. With the effortless spontaneity of a Siddha Guru, Gurumayi has created a beautiful, powerful body of poetry, which invites us in turn to dance with her. May your entry into this glorious dance with a great Master provide you with abundant joy and insight.

Stephen Fredman
Professor of English
University of Notre Dame
AUGUST 1998

Smile, Smile, Smile!

The Dwelling of the Radiant Being

The dwelling of the radiant Being
    is the true shrine of worship.
Your sincere and devotional feeling
    makes the radiant One manifest.
Sit by a pond and observe it with a pure heart —
    it becomes a pool of nectar,
    filled with beautiful lotuses.
Pick up a little stone and look at it with love —
    divine rays appear, streaming out of it.
Listen to an elder with loving attention —
    she appears as a Goddess,
    showering compassionate wisdom.

Don't go too far searching for this divine dwelling.
Don't work too hard to create such an abode.
Don't fight a battle to reclaim a pure shrine.
Don't waste your time looking for lost sacred places.
Don't tear up a garden to re-establish your faith.
Don't feel hopeless about your ability
    to acquire higher knowledge.

Look deep into yourself with contentment.
There the radiant Being dwells
    and will reveal to you its full glory.
Hold this truth in your awareness,
    and let it be suffused with true devotion.

When I Become Aware of Time

When I become aware of Time,
    the profound power
    of my Guru's compassion
      simply melts my heart
      into luminous nectar.
The sanctity, the divinity,
    of the Guru's command
      becomes as clear as a crystal
      to the eye of morning.

Everything that makes life precious and blessed
    is nourished by the Guru's knowledge.
Each second of my life scintillates
    with the effulgence of the Guru's grace.
Each inbreath and outbreath arises
    from the pulse of the Guru's *mantra.*
Every move my body makes is infused
    with the pure sweet intention
    of my Guru's will.

When I become aware of Time,
    an extraordinary sense of freedom
    rushes through my spirit.
I am given the wondrous opportunity
    to live life fully again and again.
The kindness of Time grants me
    a million exhilarating reasons
    to rejoice and let my heart sing
    the Guru's sacred name.

When I become aware of Time,
    when the sun has set
      and the stars begin to throb brightly,
    when the sun has risen
      and the world begins its myriad transactions,
    when the moon has risen
      and the herbs become receptive,
    when the moon has set
      and the brahmins begin a new cycle
      of worship,

Then I visualize
     my Shri Guru's blessed form,
     my Shri Guru's blessed eyes,
     my Shri Guru's blessed hands,
     my Shri Guru's blessed feet.
My Shri Guru's blessed voice,
     deep and strong,
     melodious and penetrating,
     resonates in my being.

Here in my Guru's presence,
     Time stands still
     and sheds all illusions.
Ethereal and serene, the blue light
     from the Guru's form
     pervades the vastness
     of all that is.

Whatever You Invest in Time

O my dear soul, keep in mind
    that whatever you invest in Time,
    you will see the exact interest.
In time you will reap the harvest
    of whatever you think, say or do.

You alone
    are responsible for your destiny.
This is the age-old truth
    that even Time cannot change.
This is not an old wives' tale
    or a superstitious yarn.
It is the wisdom of the universe.
To know this
    is to roam freely in Shiva's garden.

There is no greater witness
    than your true friend, Time.
Every vow that you make
    is observed by Time.
Whatever you possess or lack
    depends upon Time.
Respect this precious Time,
    it is on your side.

God's Power

God's power
coursing through the universe —
    What a song it composes!
    What a dance it enacts!
    What a vision it offers!

God's power
just a tiny little throb,
    and suddenly
    planets, stars and galaxies —
    mysterious universes,
    inconceivable, inaccessible —
      sprang into being.

God's power
how does it really expand?
    How does it really contract?
    How does it reveal itself?
    How does it keep itself hidden?

God's power
so overwhelmingly immense,
   so cosily nestled in the heart,
   so easily within one's reach,
   so far beyond one's grasp.

God's power
the sages say
   is benevolent to noble souls,
   terrifying to the evil-minded,
   beautiful and sweet to the devoted,
      and is everything to those who seek the truth.

A Person Whose Mind Is Steadfast

A person whose mind is steadfast
    has power over its fluctuations.
He can perceive when the mind is playing tricks
    and wallowing in negative *vṛttis*.
He is aware of the benefits
    that he harvests from spiritual practices.
He understands benevolence
    and lets it suffuse his entire being.
A steadfast mind is the fruit of *tapasyā*,
    and it brings sweet harmony within and without.

A person whose mind is steadfast
    continually labours to strengthen this virtue.
He watches which thoughts disturb his state
    and which thoughts undermine it.
He observes what he says in conversations
    and how he treats himself.
He knows that even when he is alone,
    the Guru is not separate from him.
Even in the privacy of his own mind,
    he sees virtue in others and not their faults.

A person whose mind is steadfast
    lets divine light nurture his spirit.
This brings the invaluable merit
    of constantly perceiving God's presence.
He is careful not to estrange others
    with outer shows of devotion
    that they might not understand.
He respects other people's time and energy,
    and doesn't make himself the centre of attention.
He is always willing to let go
    of what no longer has purpose.

A person whose mind is steadfast
    is very grounded on the spiritual path.
He keeps his attention on the Guru's feet
    and remembers not to harm them.
He is intent on the welfare of others,
    for he knows that the Guru's *śakti* abides in all hearts.

He relishes all forms of *prasād* from the Guru
    and doesn't try to analyse their value.
He is no fool and knows their true worth:
    they will give him liberation.

The Zenith of Your Aspirations

The zenith of your aspirations
    is so brilliantly present in each step you take —
    to experience it is to drink the nectar from a flower
    that is right before you.

If you are always rushing to the summit,
    how can you gather
    the beautiful, essential lessons
    that blossom along the way?

If your only aim is success,
    you may end up feeling like a failure.
If you are just looking for satisfaction,
    you may find yourself as famished as a ghost.
If you are busy designing your ladder to the top,
    don't be surprised
    if your peace of mind plummets.

The sky is the limit, or so we hear,
  but experience tells us
  there is something beyond.
Each mountain range in the Himalayas
  takes you higher and higher.
Yet, even after climbing the highest mountain,
  your heart, your spirit, can soar even further.
The zenith of your aspirations
  is as close as your breath
  and as infinite as the universe.

Setting a New Direction

Setting a new direction
> exceeds the reach of the intellect.

Steady self-examination
> gives you access to your own soul.

Deep inside the cave of your heart
> you receive unmistakable guidance.

By following the beam of its light
> you comprehend the heart's desires.

Otherwise, you steer your life
> by the impulses of the senses;
> there is no self-control, no sensible decision,
> just endless striving to satisfy restless ambition.

The scriptures have set forth
> clear directions for all seekers.

Read them, study them, imbibe them,
> and choose a direction
> to reach the highest goal.

There will be times, unforeseen,
        when you will need the Guru's guidance.
Don't get stuck in any one pattern;
        remain open and humble,
        without binding notions.

You may think it is you
        who is setting a new direction.
Truly, however, it is God
        who is shedding light on your path.
Sometimes, midstream, you are forced
        to find a new direction.
Look deep into your heart;
        it already knows the way.
The truth is,
        your heart is already there.

Inner Strength
Is a Gift From the Lord

Inner strength is a gift from the Lord.
It holds everything in place,
>inside and out.
It allows both change and the unchanging
>to take place.
Depending on the circumstances,
>it allows you to give in or to hold back.
Flexibility and rigidity are well-timed
>when you rely on your God-given inner strength.
This strength isn't built with the power of clever words,
>nor does it come from the support of others.
It doesn't depend on a nurturing upbringing,
>nor does it lean on your accomplishments.

To understand the greatness of this strength,
>learn to ride the golden vehicle of your own breath.
It will take you on a mystical inner journey
>and reveal to you the real treasure of life.
When you behold and touch this inner strength,
>you experience new blood
>coursing through your body.
Very soon you discover an amazing thing:
>the Lord did not just give you something small;
He placed his own lustrous, tranquil energy
>within your being — you are His work of art!

When you forget the treasure hidden in your own house,
    you begin pillaging this beautiful planet.
How then can you ever realize the true reason for living?
Just as a geologist digs up the earth
        to solve the mysteries of the universe,
        first explore your own being.

Believing you to be a seeker of the truth,
        I invite you to go on a pilgrimage to the Self.
There you will find the great untold inner strength,
        which is yours, was yours,
        and will always be yours.
Then as the rays of your joy illuminate the universe,
        you can live with total conviction.
To draw the power of the inner strength with each breath
        is to pay homage to the great Lord.

With Each New Beginning

With each new beginning
    realize the power of resolution.
Whatever your feelings may be,
    understand their cause.
When there is no more compromising,
    no more disguising,
       you can fulfil your promises.

Learn the art of going deeper into yourself,
    and come to recognize
    the true source of surrender.
Peace permeates every star
    and speck of dust.
It cannot stay only on the crust
    of the material world.
Whatever comes, let it be —
    just begin everything anew.
Your eyes will fall on God's smile.
Take a fresh breath of air
    and let your heart swell with joy.
Every time the breath comes in
    and the breath goes out,
       know it is a new beginning.

With each new beginning
    bring yourself to the awareness of God.

Secret Wish

Secret wish . . . *shhhhhhh,*
>   what am I hearing?
It is so soft — a soft whisper.
>   Who is speaking?
Everything is quiet and dark;
>   it is a moonless night.
No one seems to be out and about,
>   but the air is so full.
Aaahh. It must be a secret wish
>   that I hear as a soft whisper.

The secret wish of a ladybug,
>   what could it be?
The secret wish of a snail,
>   what could it be?
The secret wish of a grasshopper,
>   what could it be?
The secret wish of a little fish,
>   what could it be?
The secret wish of a mountain lion,
>   what could it be?
The secret wish of a lizard,
>   what could it be?
The secret wish of a giraffe,
>   what could it be?
The secret wish of a woodpecker,
>   what could it be?

The secret wish of a cardinal,
    what could it be?
The secret wish of a toddler,
    what could it be?
The secret wish of a grandmother,
    what could it be?
The secret wish of a cobra,
    what could it be?
The secret wish of a parrot,
    what could it be?
The secret wish of a tree,
    what could it be?
The secret wish of a cactus,
    what could it be?
The secret wish of a pumpkin,
    what could it be?
The secret wish of a yellow rose,
    what could it be?
The secret wish of a river,
    what could it be?

Ask yourself:
What is the secret wish of my own soul?
    Will I ever really know?
    Is it something I made up?
    Is it something God put there?

Will I make it come true?
Will it just reveal itself?
Will I recognize it?
Is it just for me?
Does it have to include everyone?
Is it — well, what is it?
Will my eagerness
make it disappear?

Oh, the secret wish of God,
what could it be?

What if we are the manifestations
of His secret wish?
Could it be?
He laughed and out we came, dancing,
while His being continued to vibrate?

Ho, ho! The secret wish of God
is now out in the open!
We are His joyful manifestations!
How must we conduct ourselves?
If He kept us as His secret wish,
how much He must have treasured us!
His love, respect and care for us
must be tremendous, immense.
We must be His precious souls.
What a wonderful Master He is!

He let His secret wish be known.
What an act of generosity!
He set us free to breathe His air
and to behold His great play.
He has given us everything.
What must His secret wish be now?

God's secret wish . . .
Could it be . . .
for us to love one another
and see His light in everyone and everything?
for us to respect one another
and help one another to experience His love?
The sages and great souls
must be His powerful messengers,
sent to deliver His secret wish.
Shall we pay attention to their guidance
and follow in their footsteps?
Won't our lives be filled
with God's smiles and God's wisdom?

My secret wish must have been
to have the great good fortune
to fulfil His secret wish
through my mind, body and soul.

Listen, dawn has arrived.
Night has vanished.
We must gently arise
    and walk towards the Sun God.

Let us refresh our resolution
    and smile at our destiny.
Let us go and offer our service
    to humanity.
We will meet again
    and revel in the wonders
    of our secret wish.

To Make a Resolution

To make a resolution
    is to abide by your heart's wishes.
When you redefine your life,
    you must revisit your intentions.
It is one thing to daydream
    and another thing to act on your decisions.
Each person has the chance
    to rephrase his own thoughts.
What is a resolution
    but a golden opportunity
    to rediscover the best solution?

To make a resolution
    is to draw a great blessing —
    you express the goodness
    of your own heart.

The Setting Sun Rejoices

The setting sun rejoices
when you put away all concerns
    and become absorbed in God's splendour,
when you respect the sacred hour of prayer
    and let your heart sing His glory,
when you begin to count your blessings
    and allow the sweetness of gratitude
    to spread through your being,
when you let the world know that it is precious
    and you will endeavour to preserve its magnificence,
when you refresh your resolution
    and smile at your destiny.

Then, when you are at one with your heart,
    the setting sun rejoices.

The Light of Your Awareness

The light of your awareness
    is a glorious boon from God.
It is your protection, your guide,
    your wealth, your liberation.
When you lose an object in the dark,
    you can find it with a candle
    or a flashlight. You can turn on a lamp.
But when you lose your thoughts,
    ideas, intentions and goals
    in the dark field of your mind,
    how will you regain them?
Only the light of your awareness
    can illumine the field of your mind.

When you are cold,
    you can sit in front of a fireplace.
The heat removes
    the chill of the body.
At the sight of the dancing flames,
    sadness melts away.
You are warm and happy again.

But when you are cold deep inside yourself,
       sad in every corner of your spirit,
       how can you reclaim the kingdom
       of warmth and joy?
Only through the light of your awareness
       can you experience the warmth of the soul,
       the bliss of the Self.

When you are down and out,
       imagining that you have fallen from grace,
       beating yourself up, raging at the Guru,
       cursing the world, bemoaning your destiny
       and losing all hope,
       you will attract the kind of people,
       you will experience the kind of circumstances
           that will only serve to reinforce
           the misery of your plight.

But with even a tiny flicker
       of the powerful light of awareness,
       you can pass through the wall of delusion.
That light is your saving grace.

The light of awareness
    is the golden column of light
    that eternally coruscates within you.
It is the central pillar
    that steadies you on the spiritual path.
It allows you to re-examine yourself
    and strengthens your faith.
It burns up impurities
    and releases higher knowledge.
It removes non-essential concerns
    and replenishes you with the essence
    of your true goal in life.
If you pay attention to its beneficent presence,
    you cross the ocean of worldliness.

How do you continue to increase
    the light of awareness
    that *śaktipāt* rekindled?

Spiritual practices are the means.
They keep this glowing light
    in the foreground of your mind
    and allow you to see by its rays.
When the Guru has charged
    each of your spiritual practices
    with great power,
    you should embrace each one fully,
      just as you would cling to a raft
      in a stormy ocean.

Even when everything seems to be going well in life,
    you mustn't forget the value
    of spiritual practices.
Only when you let yourself bathe
    in the light of awareness
    can you truly hear the Guru's loving words.
Otherwise, just like dead skin
    that has lost all sensation,
    you won't feel the power of grace
      even if the Guru touches you.

The light of awareness infuses you
        with new energy.
Very naturally, it refreshes your resolution
        and keeps you on the path.
In difficult times, it stops you
        from reaching for poison
        in the guise of pleasure.
It brings you back to drink
        from the fountain of wisdom
        that flows in your heart.
Then you can smile at your destiny.

A resolution that is constantly refreshed
        in the light of awareness
        becomes a beacon
        for those who are floundering in *māyā*.
The light of your own awareness
        is your precious companion.
Hold on to it for dear life
        and put it to beneficial use.

The light of your awareness
    is a beautiful world of its own.
When you become aware of God within,
    your whole life takes on a different hue.
The Guru's gift of *śaktipāt*
    brings the awareness
    of your own true nature.
The light of this awareness
    illumines the worlds, inside and out.

Who can measure God's greatness?
How can you count His blessings?
Worship and love Him. Become His
    through the light of your awareness.
Bring your resolution
    into the light of your awareness;
    let it come to life there.
If it can withstand the light,
    keep it and cherish it.
If it shrinks from it,
    renounce it and let it go.
As long as the light of your awareness
    refreshes your resolution,
    you will find every reason
      to smile at your destiny.

When Light Penetrates Darkness

When light penetrates darkness,
    heaven rejoices and showers nectar.
The light of your awareness
    illumines your path through life.

How can you maintain its effulgence?
How do you take its divine help?
How will you make the most of its power?

When someone harbours thoughts about you
    that are of a tamasic nature,
      let them burn up in the light of your awareness.
Only the pure essence of those thoughts will remain.
You will benefit from it.

When someone speaks words about you
    that are of a tamasic nature,
      let them be consumed by the light of your awareness.
Only the pure essence of those words will remain.
You will benefit from it.

When someone directs actions towards you
      that are of a tamasic nature,
      let them burn in the light of your awareness.
Only the pure essence of those actions will remain.
You will benefit from it.

Let the light of your awareness
      become more and more luminous.
Let it reveal to you the brightness of the day
      and the velvety darkness of the night.
When you know the supreme Light,
      you experience the true comfort of the heart.
Don't be allured by light that merely glitters
      nor be fooled by apparent darkness.
Let the light of your awareness
      nurture the very essence of your being.

The Fruit of
Refreshing Your Resolution

The fruit of refreshing your resolution
    is to experience your heart of gold.
It gives you a greater chance to reclaim
    whatever you can change.
It won't allow you to get completely lost
    in trying to bring back the past.
It takes away the feeling of helplessness
    and infuses you with fresh energy.
It helps you become aware of your power
    to make a beneficial decision.
It supports you in all your endeavours
    to blaze a trail towards goodness.
However, you must be very clear about your resolution;
    it must be for the welfare of all.

The resolution you refresh
    cannot come from animosity or ill will.
If it does, you are misusing the nectar of resolve
    to bring about everyone's abasement.
The fruit of refreshing this kind of resolution
    is utter disaster.

A resolution must be refreshed
      for your own upliftment
      and for the betterment of humankind.

Let yourself perceive the shining examples of those
      who renew their resolution
      and make a difference in this world.
Then the fruit of refreshing your resolution
      will give deeper meaning to your life.
It will be exactly
      that which you are seeking.

A Heart Resolved

A heart resolved
     on abiding in the pure space of the heart
     is continually refreshed and renewed
     by this deep intention.

Why is the moon
     ever so fresh,
     ever so exquisite,
     ever so energetic,
     ever so enthralling,
     and ever so simply beautiful?

Why is the morning mist rising over the lake
     ever so gentle,
     ever so graceful,
     ever so refreshing,
     and ever so amazingly light?

Why are the words of saints
     ever so lovely,
     ever so strong,
     ever so life-transforming,
     and ever so meaningful to true seekers?

Remember and reflect on everything
  that is pure,
  beneficial,
  beautiful,
  wondrous,
  and ever so close to your heart.

Reflect on all that touches you
  and awakens your awareness
  to divinity and simplicity.

A heart resolved
  on looking at life through God's eyes
  can see only the supreme light
    in sentient beings
    and in insentient objects.

A heart resolved
  leads to a fulfilled life.

In the Presence of Grace

In the presence of grace,
    all confusion melts away.
Deep tranquillity surges,
    the mind grows still.
Impressions from ages ago
    can find no footing.
Ancient negative tendencies
    are rendered powerless.

In the presence of grace,
    pretence slinks into oblivion.
Simplicity and humility emerge,
    the heart becomes ecstatic.

In the presence of grace,
    time stands still.
The veil of ignorance drops away,
    light comes streaming in.
One's whole being becomes luminous,
    the inner sound is audible.
The individual soul merges
    into the Great One.

In the presence of grace,
    refresh your resolution.
In the presence of grace,
    smile at your destiny.

Through the Eye of the Heart

Through the eye of the heart
  you can perceive what is hidden
  from the physical eyes.
This eye is God's eye, the Witness.
You see it in your meditation:
    it is exquisite and full of knowledge;
    it is full of love and compassion.
The *darśan* of the eye of the heart
    purifies your entire being.
When you allow your thoughts to confer with it,
    you have brighter inspirations.

The eye of the heart, your inner radar,
    will never let you down.
It won't let you berate your destiny,
    nor will it let you belittle yourself.
It won't dismiss the good person that you are,
    nor will it let you throw away
    the blessings in your life.
It is your true witness,
    the one who guides and supports you
    as you travel through the labyrinth
    of human existence.

It is there to empower your awareness
        with the real beauty and purpose
        of this universe.
From time to time
        you may even have a strong suspicion
        that someone else
        is seeing through your eyes.

We worship Shiva's third eye,
        it is the eye of the heart,
        the embodiment of grace.
When you examine each resolution
        through the eye of the heart,
        you see a very powerful image
        of what you are
        and of what you have made of yourself.
The heart is a very intelligent force.

The eye of the heart
      is on your side.
Therefore, welcome its insights.
While you chant, pray to the heart
      to reveal its clear perception.
As you go about your daily duties,
         let its gaze fall
         on each thought, word and action.
Without judging yourself,
         let the eye of the heart
         manifest your divinity.
Instead of trying to see everything
         through the prism of the mind,
         let the brilliant rays
         of the eye of the heart
         reflect everything in its true colours.

Through the eye of the heart,
      you can perceive God's throne.

Truly, Nature Abounds with Miracles

Truly, Nature abounds with miracles:
>   so it is written by all the oracles.
To find a miracle, you needn't run in circles,
>   just turn around — everything smiles.

When Nature holds such inconceivable mystery,
>   when all that she gives is so nourishing,
>   when everything she does is for the good
>   of this planet,
>   why then do human beings waste so much time
>   in experiments?

There are friendly and ferocious animals,
>   Nature carries honey and poison.
Whatever she offers benefits all.
Why then do human beings ignore her generosity?

Just because the trees don't talk back
>   when they are mercilessly hacked to pieces,
>   just because birds cannot cry for our help,
>   do human beings have the right to act recklessly?

Even the money that humans seek
    is made from the body of this earth.
Nature bestows every scrap of paper,
    every ounce of metal.
Why then do human beings fight
    over each plot of land?

Without the great healing quality of Nature,
    no lover can find true solace in a beloved,
    no stranger can make his way home.
Why then don't human beings really take care of her?

Truly, Nature abounds with enchanting smiles,
    beckoning you to release your melodious voices,
    removing the deep sorrows from your wounds.
Why then have human beings become so silent
    in the face of her destruction?

A Genuine Smile
Makes This World a Better Paradise

A genuine smile makes this world a better paradise.
Everyone aspires to be the best and most authentic.
However, people seek to uplift themselves
     in ways that do not always coincide
     with their heart's intention.

When your thoughts don't match your actions
     nor your actions fit your thoughts,
     when your thoughts don't match your words
     and your words contradict your actions,
      how genuine can your smile be?
How can you synchronize your smile
     with the goodness of your heart?

A genuine smile is the fruit of genuine effort.
Think well, speak well, and do well —
  wherever you turn
  something good will happen.
Do not expect your emotions to be pampered.
Let your heart rule the day and night.
Touch your destiny
  with a genuine smile,
  and your destiny will joyfully return your smile.

When God Smiles

When God smiles,
    the force of all forces,
    the *sahasrāra*, throbs.
The effect of the sound
    showers nectar.
The light of all lights
    infuses the field of the body,
    which responds with exultation.
The light spreads all around,
    penetrates deep within,
    uproots darkness,
    and quickens the inner light.
The seeds of good actions,
    the seeds of bad actions
    are burnt in this light.

What happens now?
Surprise of all surprises —
    the marriage of light with light,
    the dance of joy with joy,
    the song of love to love
    — this life in God's world!
No more courting mortality,
    just roaming in the immortal Self!

When God smiles,
> the *cakras* bloom,
> the *ājñācakra* shimmers,
> the *sahasrāra* shines,
> the blood cells twinkle,
> the body delights,
> the heart sings,
> the hands support,
>> the great energy permeates.

All is well.
Truth triumphs.
Love prevails.
Goodness takes over.
You refresh your resolution
> and smile at your destiny!

The Nature of the Goddess Surpasses the Mind

The nature of the Goddess surpasses the mind.
So says the *Śrī Sūkta*, describing Her being.
Only the heart can discern Her awesome power.
The Goddess yields this power uniquely
    for the well-being and protection
    of those who uplift this world.
She wipes away the darkness of an ignorant mind
    and snatches away the desire to harm others.
She realigns the mind, spirit and body
    so that they recognize and reflect
    the supreme indwelling Lord.

When you perceive Her and Her actions
    through an untested, unpurified mind,
    She may appear quite distorted.
She may seem terrifying,
    a source of primal fear,
    the incarnation of doom,
    and the mind will do anything to protect itself.
But a heart that is at peace and content in its own light
    perceives Her immense beauty and compassion,
    and strives to embrace Her, to merge with Her.

The heart delights in beholding Her luminous presence
      in loveliness and ugliness,
      in agreement and discord,
      in health and death,
      in laughter and derision,
      in good times and bad times,
      in each moment now and evermore.
Only if the mind can follow Her to the very end
      will it find itself
      in a scintillating, enchanted garden,
      the heavenly garden where divine light
      absorbs every atom
      and regenerates Consciousness
        out of its own being.

Wonderstruck As I Watch

I am wonderstruck as I watch
  your blazing light, O my lovely moon;
completely lost as I behold
  your amazing beauty, O my lovely moon.

Suddenly, O my lovely moon,
  I am awakened to your presence,
as I become aware of how silently
  you rose over the shining hills.

Intoxication runs through my blood
  as each cell of my being
sings your unparalleled glory
  and I remain only a pure witness.

"You are just so unassuming"
  is what I think, then wonder,
"How can you blaze so brilliantly
  and so unassumingly all at once?"

How mysterious and beautiful you are,
  always smiling — not just in the sky
but also in the secret chamber of my heart.
  And I realize you are the magic of my life.

Lost in Supreme Bliss

Lost in supreme bliss,
>   he made me find my own Self.
He is my most adorable Lord,
>   to whom I owe my whole life.
He is my Babaji,
>   he is my radiant Guru.
He made me realize that everything but the Self
>   is a tenacious noose.

With his eyes in *śāmbhavīmudrā*,
>   he opened my eyes to the world of light.
By breathing the same air,
>   he purified my environment.
With his lionlike roar,
>   he scared away my inner enemies.
He constantly dwelt in *yogabhūmi*
>   and spread its energy everywhere.

Lost in supreme bliss,
>   he redeemed seekers from falling into the abyss.
He taught us all
>   to open our hearts and fly.
Freedom is his abode;
>   that is why he abides in our hearts.

Destiny, the Mystery of Mysteries

Destiny, the mystery of mysteries,
   the wonder of great wonders.
Who can decode her enigma?
Now, at this very moment,
   are you influenced by your destiny?
Can you smile at a destiny
   you do not comprehend?
Are you extolling its greatness?
Do you admire your own destiny?
Do you find it interesting?
Do you believe you have a destiny?
Are you afraid of the intricate web
   that your destiny has spun?
Are you running away from your destiny?

Does your destiny look as beautiful, as spectacular
   as a rainbow?
Or does your destiny feel like you're washing
   a white cloth in muddy water?

Whatever the case may be for you,
   your life is already in tremendous motion.
Whether you will it or not,
   right before your eyes
   life just continues to happen.

Yet there is no reason to be elated or sad.
External appearances do not matter.
Destiny does not just occur
     on the surface of your existence.
It is the inner world that has the true power.

Embrace the Guru's grace completely.
It yields the sweetest fruit.
The heart that has been touched by the Guru's love
     is studded with the gems of shining virtues.
The Guru's compassionate and tender glance can give you
     a greater view of your destiny.
Then you know you are neither crunched
     by the sharp jaws of your destiny
     nor garlanded by it.
Your destiny does not control you.

Kuṇḍaliniśakti is awake and at work.
The *sahasrāra* is blazing with ethereal light.
The eyes have been pierced by the Guru's *śāmbhavīmudrā*.
The heart is established in the *turīya* state.
Everything is a play of Consciousness.
Everywhere you see the soul's perfection.

Destiny — what destiny?
Mystery — what mystery?
O life, can't you see —
    there is nothing but scintillating particles
    of supreme Consciousness.

Hail to Shri Guru,
    whose one look,
    one word,
    and one touch
    has transformed my unfathomable destiny
    into this sacred and golden dust
    befitting the abode of his luminous lotus feet.

Hail to Shri Guru,
    whose supreme compassion continues to allow me
    to drink the fragrant nectar of love
    from his unending reservoir
    of the melodious and primordial *Om*.

Hail to Shri Guru,
    who has unlocked
    the inscrutable shackles of my destiny
    and set me free to roam
    in his splendid, immaculate, ecstatic,
    vast, deep, wisdom-filled,
    grace-bestowing realm.

Hail to Shri Guru,
    who has absorbed my destiny,
    my limitations, my life
    into his own being
    and made me his own.

To belong to my Shri Guru,
    to be fashioned by his own hands,
    to be nurtured by his love,
    to merge into his light
    is my destiny.

This is my great good fortune,
    and my Guru has bestowed this *prasād* upon me.
Therefore, my destiny
    is my Guru's supreme gift.
May I always remember:
    my sustenance is my Guru's lotus feet.

When There Is True Love

When there is true love,
    what more can you ask for?
Wherever a king goes,
    his retinue accompanies him.
Whatever he needs on the journey
    is carefully provided for him.
In the same way,
    when there is true love,
    God's kingdom manifests before your eyes.
Everything you need smiles at you.
You just know you are love,
    you don't question or analyse it.
True love places you in the best seat
    in God's kingdom.

How do you convey this love to others?
Here great discipline is needed.
Do you just talk about it
    or write about it
    or let others imagine it?
Do you paint your true love abstractly
    and hope others will get it?
Do you try to hide it
    and make others wonder about it?

Do you boast about it,
    parade it around,
    and make others feel less special?
Do you overpower others
    and undermine them
    until they beg you for it?
Do you sneer at others
    for their lack of depth in love?
Do you think that silence
    is the way to express your love?
Do you walk around pretending
    you have never really experienced it?
How do you share this true love?
Would you rather hoard it for yourself?

When there is true love,
    nothing matters but its radiance.
It can only do good.
When there is true love,
    your only wish
    is to give it to the world.
How can the majestic banyan tree
    hide its roots?

Your Sweet Smile

Your sweet smile sparkles
  in each strand of this universe.
Its power sometimes ushers,
  sometimes thrusts me into my heart.

How amazing and magical
  is this ethereal abode,
  in which your divine will is treasured!

My heart is your home,
  your true, sweet home,
A cave that welcomes me to stay,
  to linger within it forever.

From this divine abode
  everything is perceived so clearly:
  the sudden flash of the lustrous Blue Pearl,
  the spreading petals of the immortal flower,
  the subtle movement of the *kuṇḍalinīśakti*,
  the squeal of a delighted child,
  the unspoken gratitude of a devotee,
  the bright eyes of a beggar,
  the melodious sound of the *mantra*,
  the eager stance of a merchant,

the habitual discontent of a taxi driver,
the gentle and undeniable hunger for food,
the thirst that only the scriptures can quench,
the duty to serve humanity,
the iridescent arch of a rainbow,
the longing of a cornfield reaching for the sky,
the sweetness of a caring friend,
the strong pull of meditation,
the intoxication of a dancing *saptāḥ*,
the golden crescent rising in the early morning.

Only by remaining in the heart
    can I truly perceive
    the wonders that flow
    from the gift of your smile.

Your sweet smile
    spreads from east to west,
    from north to south —
    farther than the east,
    farther than the west,
    farther than the north,
    farther than the south.

Your smile is my heart.
Your smile is my life.
Your smile is my destiny.
So I smile at my destiny — it is perfect!

May your sweet smile be the foundation
    of my thoughts, words and actions.
May only joy sprout everywhere.
May only love spread everywhere.
May only peace abound everywhere.
May your sweet smile be
    the lasting principle
    in my world.

With a Fresh Young Spirit

With a fresh young spirit
 roam the mystical and sacred land.
Youth, freshness and spirit
 are each cherished and admired.
When you put them all together
 and enter the subtle realm,
  you see a world beyond imagination.
Ecstasy, wisdom, light and serenity
 permeate the four directions.
Music runs through the velvety fabric
 of this uncovered ground.
Uncrowded, clear,
 its spirit is always fresh,
 reborn in each moment.

Come, my dear soul!
 You and I have an open invitation
 to experience our own fresh young spirit.
Let us make this our true offering to God,
 whose grace takes us
 to the feet of the Master.

Great Blessings Always Come

Great blessings always come.
Only a heart drenched with peace
    knows this certainty.
Great blessings carry hidden treasures —
    exactly the ones you need.
A seeker must know how to preserve them
    in a heart that is sacred and serene.

A pot of gold may be hidden
    at the end of a rainbow,
    but the path of *sādhanā*
    is strewn with blessings
    all along the way.
As you make progress you gather them,
    and they continue to enrich you
    with ever-increasing enthusiasm.
You move on with the firm resolution
    to protect all the great blessings
    that have been bestowed upon you.
You become increasingly worthy to receive them.

Your heart smiles
     as you inhale the fragrance
     of these great blessings.
Then you never need to prove yourself,
     nor do you need to brag.
You don't have to hide yourself;
     you don't need to be jealous of others.

Great blessings always come
     with a genuine smile.
Your heart is affected by their power,
     and your whole being bows
     with deep humility.
And that, too, is a great blessing.

Show Me the Way

Sitting beside a beautiful lake
　　wondering about your resolution,
　　reflecting on your destiny
　　you pray to the Lord.
Show me the way.
Please show me the way.

How do I find the holy river
　　by bathing in which I can refresh my resolution
　　and feel pure enough to smile at my destiny?

How do I find the sacred tree
　　by standing under which I can refresh my resolution
　　and feel moved to smile at my destiny?

How do I find the sacred stone
　　by holding which I can refresh my resolution
　　and feel free to smile at my destiny?

How do I find the holy mountain
　　by climbing which I can refresh my resolution
　　and accept the power to smile at my destiny?

How do I find the pot of gold
　　in which I can dip my resolution,
　　helping me to perceive the world with a fresh outlook
　　and smile at my destiny?

How do I find the paradise
     by abiding in which I can refresh my resolution
     and discover the pleasure of smiling at my destiny?

How do I find the holy text
     by reciting which I can refresh my resolution
     and become wise enough to smile at my destiny?

How do I find the sacred space
     by entering which I can refresh my resolution
     and know the wish to smile at my destiny?

How do I find the auspicious time
     by staying in which I can refresh my resolution
     and shine with the lustre to smile at my destiny?

How do I find a quiet mind
     in whose serenity I can refresh my resolution
     and experience the grace to smile at my destiny?

How do I find the voice of God
     by hearing which I can refresh my resolution
     and become eager to smile at my destiny?

How do I find the command of my Guru
     by learning which I can refresh my resolution
     and surrender to smiling at my destiny?

How do I find the source of the universe
  by knowing which I can refresh my resolution
  and revive the desire to smile at my destiny?

How do I find the colour of all colours
  by dyeing myself in which I can refresh my resolution
  and gain the inspiration to smile at my destiny?

The brightness of the day is too intense.
The darkness of the night is too profound.
My resolution continues to wax and wane.
If it doesn't remain steady, how can I refresh it?
What reason will I have to smile at my destiny?

If I keep wandering, won't I get lost?
If I remain in one place, won't I get stuck?
If I keep searching, won't I lose faith?
If I stop midstream, won't I drown?

The questions grow in number
  as my resolution waits to be refreshed.
The answers seem out of reach
  as I try hard to smile at my destiny.

O Lord of Lords, show me the way
    to refresh my resolution
    and smile at my destiny.
Show me the way.
I pray, show me the way.

My Dear One,
There is nowhere to look but deep in your heart.
There is nothing to touch but the depths of your heart.
There is nothing to hear but the song of your heart.
There is nothing to taste but the sweetness of your heart.
There is nothing to inhale but the fragrance of your heart.

Within you, I untie the knot of the heart.
Allow yourself to be drawn into the heart's effulgence.
Let your resolution be absorbed by its power,
    and you can perceive the heart's resolve.

Behold your supreme glory as you smile at your destiny!

With Songs and Laughter

With songs and laughter,
    so gently you touched something
    very deep inside me, my Lord.
Now, with songs and laughter,
    I open the door for you, my Lord.
Night and day I'll stay awake
    just to serve you with all my love.
Oh yes, this is my great vow.

Now, very humbly I ask for your grace.
May I never forget you,
    the great Lord who is before my eyes.
May I always remember
    your gentle, guiding hand.
May I keep my heart
    secure at your golden lotus feet.
May I sing your glory
    and spread the fragrance of your name.
May I rejoice in your laughter
    and spread the nectar of your ecstasy.

O my dear ones, with songs and laughter,
    say goodbye to the old life.
With songs and laughter,
    choose a divine life in God's service.
With songs and laughter,
    invite everyone to share in God's abundance.
With songs and laughter,
    create a magical world.
With songs and laughter,
    bring everyone to know their true greatness.
With songs and laughter,
    receive God's blessings.
With songs and laughter,
    embrace the Guru's grace.
Come, all of you come,
    with songs and laughter!

Refresh Your Resolution.
Smile at Your Destiny.

NEW YEAR'S MESSAGE 1998

*W*ITH GREAT RESPECT, WITH GREAT LOVE, I welcome
you all with all my heart.

It's begun! We've crossed the threshold. Here we
are in the moonlit new year of 1998. It's so new. It's so
bright. It's so transparent. It's so tender. It's so caring.
It's so mysterious. It's delightful. It's promising. It
sparkles with good humour. It is iridescent. It is melo-
dious. It is precious. It carries deep wisdom — the
moonlit new year.

When the year actually changes, what happens? We
too travel with time. It feels great, doesn't it? Time is
such a great revealer, such a wise teacher, such a glorious
asset. Time is a sweet companion and a scold. Time is a
lover. Time, is a secret. Time is the most ancient sage.
Time is ever playful, ever open and expansive. Time, the
great equalizer, resonates with the Truth.

Isn't it wonderful to travel with time? When you
flow with time, you are not rushing towards the next
event. You are not always thinking there is something
better waiting just around the bend. Nor do you drag
your feet, trying to cling to memories of the good old
days. When you are in *sync* with time, you know you are
in the right place, at the right time, and with the right
people. When you move with time, your wisdom grows
to immense proportions.

Once upon a time we woke up to our inner courage
and became steeped in divine contentment. We tasted its

nectar. We relished it. We drank to our hearts' content. We became so immersed in the delicious pool of contentment that 1998 came like a silky jasmine breeze and whispered, "I am here." And it was true! We opened our eyes and found ourselves in the moonlit new year.

On the whole, I would say we rose to the occasion. How did we do it? With the sound of God's name. We could feel it approaching from the depths of our being and vibrating through our lips: God Himself in the form of sound. Is it fire? Is it nectar? Is it velvet? Is it emptiness? Is it just what it ought to be? How can we describe the way God's presence makes itself felt? A great Sufi saint sings:

O Lord, You are my goal and You are my destiny.
You are my only aspiration and my heart's desire.
Everyone worships You, because You are the one
who is truly worthy of reverence.

Those who are blinded by ignorance
are convinced that You don't exist.
But those who have the eyes of wisdom
proclaim God is alive, You are alive.
They have seen You, O Lord.

Why should I beg from anyone?
What can anyone else give me,
when my Lord, my great Lord, gives me everything?
My Lord gives me everything
with His unseen, invisible hands.

You have such unique artistry in Your hands, O Lord.
You can create anything.
You give each one of us our life and You nurture it.
Therefore, I have put my faith in You alone.

Friends, don't embroil yourselves in petty concerns.
Absorb yourselves in chanting.
Soak your mind in God's name.
Then even the hardest times
will not be able to dampen your spirits.

If He bestows just one compassionate glance upon you,
then not only will you be uplifted,
in that moment your entire destiny will change its course.
O Lord, You are my goal and You are my destiny.

THE MOONLIT NEW YEAR: It is so refreshing, is it not? It is already full of your resolutions, is it not? And your smiles, too. It makes your destiny intriguing, does it not? Ahh, moonlit new year, you are bound to make us better than the best. You are eager to stretch our limits, to make us reach the zenith of our aspirations. Will you unite our hearts? Yes. You are prepared to draw us closer to God. Then, moonlit new year, what message do you hold for us?

The Siddha Yoga meditation message for 1998 is "Refresh your resolution. Smile at your destiny."

This message comes in the form of an expanded poem. You can think of it as a *dhāranā*. In Sanskrit, the root of the word *dhāranā* means "holding or placing something in the field of your awareness." The word *dhāranā* implies that which flows into the space within yourself, a place that is intimate and familiar and filled with unexplored possibilities. The scriptures call this space supreme Consciousness. So let your heart become a vessel to contain these words. Let your heart be completely open as we journey together through this poem.

The ancient Indian scripture called the *Atharvaveda* says:

> The person whose resolution is firm knows that the powerful Lord dwells within all beings and hears everyone's prayers. To one who inwardly offers himself to his resolution, the Lord happily gives the inner strength and equanimity to endure all hardships with a sublime and peaceful smile.

Refresh your resolution. Smile at your destiny.

With each new beginning comes a natural desire for change. We respond by setting a new direction. And so we make a resolution, a shining promise to ourselves. However, it cannot stop there. Every resolution, large or small, requires effort. It can be realized only if this effort is sustained. It needs your attention on an ongoing basis. Every resolution has to be carried out with resolution. When this is not the case, you make resolution after resolution, resolution after resolution, resolution after resolution — you have an ocean of resolutions crashing on the shores of daily life, littering your mind with broken promises. You see, a shining resolution that is not honoured will not disappear. It stays in your awareness. Like driftwood in the waves or a blinding flash of light on the water, it's always moving around trying to catch your attention. You know it's there. You become aware of your inability to act on it. You see your laziness, lack of strength, and negligence. You try to make it go away. You come up with a hundred million excuses for why you aren't willing to fulfil it. But it won't go away, because you have given life to it. There has to be some resolution about it, even if you don't want to fulfil it. Otherwise, you are the one who is going to be eaten up. Sooner or later this leads to an atmosphere of hopelessness and helplessness.

Cynicism, lack of worth, lifelessness, lack of strength: all these forms of unhappiness show up when your resolution stagnates. In this way, little by little, a person succumbs to the spirit of darkness. Therefore, it is vitally important to understand the nature of resolution.

To make a resolution is to decide on a course of action with firm determination. What impels you to make a resolution? Why do you make a resolution? Basically, there are two answers to this question: the impetus either comes from the outside or from the inside. For instance, you may decide to make a resolution because you have noticed something in your community, in your parents, or in your friends. You may have accepted standards of how to be, how to eat, what to weigh, and how to care for your body — and you resolve to achieve these goals. Resolutions like this can be positive and very sound. They can improve your experience of life if you embrace them in a sane way. Or your resolve may come from inside yourself, as a vision of your deepest wish, your sweetest dream. When you make a resolution, it is a way of drawing this secret wish into the light of your awareness and putting it into action so that your life increasingly reflects God's love, God's essence.

Whether your resolutions are practical or lofty, what matters is how you hold on to them. For a resolution to have power, you must hold it so close to your heart that it is almost like a secret, almost a prayer.

THE ANCIENT RGVEDA says:

> May you awaken like the sun at daybreak,
> ready to make your sacred offering.
> Set forth with delight, like a pilgrim on his journey.
> O heroic one, move forward with resolve
> to make this sacred offering of yourself to life.
> May you plant the banner of victory
> in the service of humankind.

This prayer is charged with resolution. Can you hear it? Can you see it? Can you feel it? Also, it conveys the fact that this resolution has to be refreshed every day. The sun never rises the same way twice: the colour of the sky, the angle of light, even the heat are all unique. And yet the whole earth is renewed. That never changes. To have the image of waking up at dawn like the sun recharges your entire being with the fresh smell of the morning earth. You can just see the birds darting out of the trees, out of the rocks, out of the bushes and flying across the rising sun, chirping. You can hear the ringing of bells at the hour of morning prayer. This is such a fulfilling way to begin the day, with *Śri Gurugītā*. It infuses the entire body with life-giving energy. Then we put that energy to use in the most beneficial way possible — in *sevā*, in the service of humanity. Refreshing your resolution — this is what enlivens resolutions that may have gone dormant. They are just sleeping, you see, waiting for the dawn. Remember, refresh your resolution.

The *Atharvaveda* says that one whose resolution is firm knows that the Lord dwells within all beings and hears everyone's prayers. Isn't that the sweetest thing you have ever heard? The Lord hears your prayers. Just hearing that — "the Lord hears your prayers" — just believing in that is so refreshing. To the person "who inwardly offers himself to his resolution, the Lord gives the inner strength to endure all hardships with a sublime and peaceful smile". Of course, the sages have taken a royal road, a golden path. They had the vision of God within everyone, and their experience became their resolution. See the power in their resolution. Their experience became their resolution. Yet even this must be refreshed. You can never become lackadaisical about the highest Truth. Like the morning sun, your resolution has to be new every day. Its colours must blaze brightly.

Nature is a master at this renewal. She knows just exactly how to refresh herself, how to rejuvenate her seeds and revamp her paradise. She refreshes herself through storms, torrents of rain, floods, brushfires, volcanoes and earthquakes. These are the most dramatic displays of the ways she renews her being. But the same process also happens on a smaller scale: like a snake shedding its skin, the trees dropping their leaves in the autumn, or a bear hibernating. Think of the way the winter snow covers the ground like a blanket; it seals in the earth's own heat so that seeds can germinate underground. Or think of an even subtler level of renewal. Think of the dew — the nightly perspiration that moistens the earth. Think of the mist rising off a lake, or delicate showers. Or think of the fact that while most of the herbs grow by the light of the sun, others are nourished by moonlight. It's amazing, isn't it? The food that sustains our life draws on all the different lights of day and night. Nature is absolutely gorgeous in her liveliness. You want to know beauty? Observe Nature. That is because she constantly refreshes her resolution and, in so doing, she refreshes the entire universe.

The fruit of refreshing your resolution is as plain as day. The energy of the entire universe supports you. You have a clear vision of the purpose of your life. You are filled with the breath of self-confidence. You experience your fresh young spirit. You make progress. Your self-esteem heightens. Listen to the fruit of your resolution. You flourish. You are bursting with inspiration. You glow with optimism. You become radiant. For you, life is dazzling with newness.

A GENUINE RESOLUTION CONTINUALLY spreads its delight all around. Why? Because it is born out of love. Does the same thing happen when a resolution is prompted by selfish motives? Not really. When a resolution is saturated with hostility, when it is spawned by bitterness or fuelled by resentment, when a resolution breeds in a swamp of inferiority, then you won't even see the shadow of ecstasy. You will not be able to experience one ounce of gladness from it. Such resolutions must *not* be refreshed. They should be burned in a funeral pyre. Let even the seeds burn completely to ashes. But a resolution that upholds what is noblest in life deserves to be honoured. It brings strength and serenity to the one who keeps faith with it. Refresh your resolution. Smile at your destiny.

There are a hundred million ways of going about this — renewing the power of your resolution, creating a transformation in your deepest commitments and convictions. Be resolute! Brighten up your resolution. Restore the positive energy in your resolution. Light a fire under your resolution.

In India, when a resolution is made — before, during, and after — you invoke Shakti, the divine power. First you create an environment of sacredness and blessedness. Then you let your resolution manifest in the most auspicious way, streaming from the inside, from the heart into speech. Then you allow it to be absorbed by the holiness of the divine power. Finally you ask for protection: you ask for the strength to sustain this resolution and live up to its merit and its excellence. Can you see the hidden force in your resolution? By verbalizing your resolution in the presence of grace, you give it a true and fresh life. That moment stirs the soul. It is like receiving initiation, *dīkṣā*. You are making a resolution, and you are also receiving *dīkṣā*. A resolution that is born out of a humble, sincere heart produces a rich and a bountiful harvest. Such a resolution must not be forgotten. It has to be refreshed over and again. It has to become like the morning sun, bringing new life to every single day. Refresh your resolution.

Baba Muktananda once said:

> If you really want to advance on the spiritual path, you have to be very firm, very resolute, and very disciplined. If you leave yourself loose, you will fall very quickly.

Everyone knows that when a bone becomes brittle, then any little accident will break it. It is no different with inner work. The way to keep your spiritual life strong and supple is through firm resolution. Otherwise, carelessness seeps in and eats away the merits of your good actions, your *punyakarma*. Your *punyakarmas* are eaten up. Before you know it, you begin to lose interest in the very things that bring you good fortune. You become indifferent to the spiritual practices that make your life meaningful. You get bored with people of good will. You distrust your friends, your good friends, who only wish for your well-being. You look upon every divine sign with suspicion. You become deadened to nature, which is the source of your life. You waste away the thousand and one boons that you have received from God. All this happens, let me tell you, very gradually, imperceptibly. You scarcely notice it. However, when your resolution becomes shaky, weakness filters into every aspect of your life.

What can you do to avert these possible disasters? Refresh your resolution. Understand the impact of a resolution. Come to see how even the simplest resolution breathes new life into you. For instance, you may have made a resolution to follow the road to good health. You may have made a resolution to take your family on a holiday when *they* want to go. You may have made a resolution to speak sweetly to others. You may have made a resolution to support good causes. You may have made a resolution to see the bright side of life. You may have made a resolution to increase your devotion. You may have made a resolution to do at least one spiritual practice a day. You may have made a resolution to give *dakṣiṇā* regularly. You may have made a resolution to see God in everyone. You may have made a resolution to experience God's protection in everything. These examples are about enhancing your life and bringing greater meaning to it.

Another approach is when you make a resolution to refrain from certain actions. You may have resolved to break the habit of constant arguing. You may have resolved to put an end to your tendency of comparing yourself with others. You may have made a resolution to stop misunderstanding Lakshmi, the goddess of wealth. Some of your resolutions may be about trivial, everyday matters, or they may be about things that are deeply meaningful to you. You may be embarrassed about some of them, even if you never tell a soul. Therefore it is very important to look at each resolution through the eye of the heart. Ask yourself, how does it go down? How does it sit inside? What is that deep feeling? Is it putting you at ease? Or is it creating havoc? Look at it from the eye of the heart. It *will* tell you the truth. Yes, the heart tells the truth.

Of course, every resolution is bound to be important to you. Otherwise, you never would have thought of it. So you must honour your resolutions — every one — small or large, pragmatic or cosmic. Whether you are praying for self-improvement or for all of mankind, your resolution matters. Never give it up. Jalal al-Din Rumi, the great Sufi mystic, says:

> Come, come, whoever you are —
> Wanderer, worshipper, fugitive.
> It doesn't matter.
> Ours is not a caravan of despair.
> Ours is a caravan of endless joy!
> Come — even if you have broken your vow
>   a thousand times.
> Come, come yet again. Come.

This is so refreshing. The call of Rumi. His words are as alive now as the day he first wrote them. And every time you read them, they give you fresh encouragement.

The truth is, you must never despair. No matter how many times you have to pick yourself up and start over, just do it. Rumi said, "Ours is not a caravan of despair." Trust his words. Believe him. "Ours is not a caravan of despair." How could it be? We have entered the moonlit year, and it holds eternal spring. Remember, it's so new. It's so bright. It's so transparent. It's so tender, so caring, so mysterious. It's delightful and promising. It sparkles with good humour. It is iridescent. It is melodious. It is precious. It carries deep wisdom—the moonlit year.

Refresh your resolution. It is like taking a dip in the Ganges at dawn and welcoming God in the form of the sun, the glorious sun. In the same way, dip your resolution in the refreshing, nectarean teachings of the scriptures. Learn to remember God. Learn to rethink each thought. Learn to reshape each action. Learn to re-examine your own heart. Learn to renew your understanding of what you have heard. Refresh your resolution. Smile at your destiny.

𝓑ABA MUKTANANDA SAYS, "One creates one's own destiny." That is a very remarkable statement, is it not? One person is born blind, another poor; another has to share his mother's womb with six other siblings. Yet, Baba says, "One creates one's own destiny." What can he possibly mean? Baba continues:

> We create our own heaven and our own hell,
> but we hold other things responsible for it, such as
> our country or our government or our destiny or our
> parents or the planets or the scheme of things.
> We become friends with one person and keep
> swaying in the joy of that friendship. We become
> hostile to another person and keep rejecting him all
> the time inside ourselves. But it is we who have creat-
> ed that friend, that enemy. Therefore, change your
> way of looking at things, make it divine. We meditate
> so that we may be able to see the world as it really is.

If, as Baba says, you are the creator of your own
destiny, then why not create it with a smile? If you are
the experiencer of your own destiny, then why not expe-
rience it with a smile? If you are the owner of your own
destiny, then why not own it with a smile? Baba says,
"Change your way of looking at things, make it divine"
—then why not look at things through the eye of the
heart? Isn't that where the divine dwells within us? If you
perceive things in this way, you will have an irresistible
impulse to smile. And guess what? It will brighten up
your destiny.

Destiny and *smile*: both of these words are practically
buzzing with nuances, connotations, histories, different
interpretations, philosophical arguments, centuries of
pessimism and optimism—the field is very crowded.
Smile and *destiny*: they are highly debatable. They have

been put through fiery tests, and yet they remain an absolute enigma. Nevertheless, your destiny continues to fashion and refashion your life, and so does your smile.

A Spanish proverb says, *Todo el mundo sonríe en el mismo idioma*: "Everyone smiles in the same language." Just think of all the ways a smile has affected you — because, of course, everyone knows there is more than one way of smiling. A smile can send your spirits soaring. A smile can be an expression of wisdom, welcome, playfulness, innocence, joy, compassion and benevolent grace.

It is one thing to receive a warm, approving smile from someone you care about very deeply, and quite another thing to receive a smile from someone who hates you, who is sarcastic, scornful and cold. That smile can cut you to the quick. In fact, a smile can be a way of showing aggression, like animals baring their teeth. What other kinds of smiles do you come across? Flirtatious, knowing, embarrassed; plastic, nervous, mischievous, and vague. And then, there is the famous smirk. There is no doubt that every type of smile has played a part in creating your destiny. However, in the end, it doesn't matter what people think about the subject of destiny; it is created.

Whether destiny is glorified or criticized, garlanded or reviled, or simply denied as a force in the universe, its basic principle is at work all the time. The truth is so simple, it is crystal clear: every action has a reaction, every cause has an effect. This is what keeps the vicious circle going. Whatever it is called — *karma,* destiny, fate, coincidence, chance, or luck, *el destino, bhāgya, prārabdha, niyati, adṛṣṭa, kismet, naseeb* — it is all the same. The naming ceremony doesn't really matter. What must happen does happen, irrespective of one's intelligence or foolishness, one's money or poverty, one's stinginess or generosity or rank in life. That is just the way it is. Goodness breeds goodness, evil breeds evil. This has been proved in every age and in every culture. Therefore, why not greet your destiny with a genuine smile, a smile like Baba's, a smile that will smooth the hard edges of destiny and empower you to move in a direction that evokes auspiciousness, *maṅgala.* A genuine smile truly opens the heart.

Describing the way Nature smiles, an author once said: "Laughter is day, and sobriety is night, and a smile is the twilight that hovers gently between both — more bewitching than either."

The bewitching smile. Truly, Nature abounds with enchanting smiles. It is our duty to learn from her. We must allow our being to absorb her offerings, so that we can give back to the universe all the golden presents that we have received, so that we learn generosity. In both word and image, the Lord is often represented with a smile playing on His lips. It is an expression of His bliss, out of which the whole world is made. The ancient *Vedas* say: "When God smiles, the sun shines, the moon glimmers, the stars twinkle, the flowers bloom."

*B*ENEVOLENT GRACE ALWAYS SMILES. Therefore, the *Śrī Sūkta* describes the awesome power of the Devi, Shakti, God's own energy, saying:

> The nature of the Goddess surpasses the mind
> and lies beyond words of mortal speech.
> Her face is lit with a beautiful smile;
> Her body is radiant with golden light.
> She is compassionate and generous.

In the same way, verse 92 of *Śrī Gurugītā* says:

> The Guru has a gentle smile (*mandasmita*).
> The Guru is joyous.
> The Guru is a treasure-house of abundant grace.

Mandasmita — the gentle smile, the soft smile, the tender smile, the caring smile, the benevolent smile. Baba Muktananda writes beautifully about the smile of his Guru, Bhagawan Nityananda:

> Lost in supreme bliss, his face was always illuminated
> with a radiant, sweet and compassionate smile. From
> time to time, he would laugh, and that laughter still
> echoes in my memory. Because he loved to smile,
> people came to address him as Nityananda, one who
> is always in bliss.

Baba inherited his Guru's smile completely. By cultivating such an open, pure and genuine smile, such a gentle and wise smile towards destiny, you are truly able to call forth your own inner divinity. Then you will not be tormented by the hot winds of the opinions of this world. A true, genuine smile is like a cool breeze. It carries the seeds of serenity and ease and scatters them over the earth, where they take root. The destiny that grows from such a smile spreads its fragrance everywhere. Smile at your destiny.

Baba says:

> One who has received true knowledge ... considers destiny to be a mere game and lives life joyfully. He knows that all kinds of things happen in life and that the world is a vale of sorrow, but he does not worry about it. Destiny does not terrify him. He remains calm in the midst of difficulties and does not get bored if life is easy.

Smile at your destiny. Isn't destiny the mystery of all mysteries? Different people have different approaches to destiny. Some people think that destiny steers their every move. Others think, "I control my destiny." Some people think that character defines destiny. You get what you are, so to speak. Others make themselves helpless victims of destiny. They think there is nothing they can do, and they give up right away. Some people resist destiny. For example, they have great things to share, but they withhold their love. Some people have an adversarial relationship with destiny. They think destiny is out to get them: "It's coming at me!" They blame destiny for all their problems. Still others refuse to believe destiny exists. But listen, destiny is knocking at the door. Whether you hear it or not, destiny opens the door by itself. Smile at your destiny.

Some people think destiny is a great teacher. There is so much to learn from it, they say. Some people actually want to work with their destiny to achieve fulfilment. Some people want to support others' destiny by being good to them. Some people have total faith in destiny. Some appeal to destiny for help. And the sages know they have a higher destiny, because they believe God dwells within themselves.

At any rate, destiny seems to play a very important role in everyone's life, believe it or not. Whether you try to face your destiny, dodge it or deny it, destiny is there in one form or another. Therefore, in Siddha Yoga meditation we always like to refer to destiny as our great good fortune, *sadbhāgya*. We say, "It is my great good fortune that I have a Guru. It is my great good fortune that I have such wonderful people in my life. It is my great good fortune that I have a longing for God." By constantly addressing it with these exalted names —

sadbhāgya, saubhāgya, puṇyakarma—we are able to smile at our destiny. And in turn, it smiles at us sweetly and generously. Great blessings always come with a genuine smile. Baba used to like the saying, "If you cry, you cry by yourself. If you laugh, the whole world laughs with you." In the same way, if you smile, you befriend the whole world. But if you complain all the time, you push everyone away. So by smiling at your destiny, you bring out the best in it. Then it doesn't matter what your destiny is—you bring out the best in destiny by smiling at it. And also, since every action has a reaction, smiling now plants the seeds of happiness for the future.

What do you think you will accomplish by berating your destiny? What do you think you will lose by smiling at it? Don't wait for a favourable change in your destiny. Smile at your destiny right now. Don't turn away from an unfavourable shift in your fortunes. Smile at your destiny. What you think is favourable may not be so great. What you think is unfavourable may be to your advantage. Therefore, smile at your destiny—whatever form it takes. Always envision your destiny as a harbinger of good news. Think like that. Smile at your destiny. Smile. As Baba says: "Be happy. Have great joy and bliss, and always smile." Make yourself a great giver of good fortune. Make yourself a refreshing lake. Make yourself an abode of fulfilling resolutions.

Refresh your resolution. Smile at your destiny. Take this message to heart, and you will fill your year with songs and laughter, with sweet fulfilment. The touch of your smile will make every facet of your destiny shimmer like the colours of a rainbow. Keep yourself very fresh and very light. With a fresh young spirit, walk the path. With a fresh young spirit, walk the path. With a fresh young spirit, walk the path. Refresh your resolution. Smile at your destiny.

With great respect, with great love, I welcome you all with all my heart.

Glossary

AJNA CHAKRA [*ājñācakra*]
The spiritual centre located between the eyebrows; known as the third eye, the seat of inner wisdom. *See also* CHAKRA.

ATHARVA VEDA [*atharvaveda*]
One of the four *Vedas*; it consists of prayers for the healing of disease and the restoration of harmony in the world, and songs celebrating the power and omniscience of God. *See also* VEDAS.

BHAVA [*bhāva*]
Attitude; emotional state; a feeling of absorption or identification.

BLUE LIGHT
An infinite expanse of resplendent blue that one may see in the inner realm during deep meditation; the colour of pure Consciousness.

BLUE PEARL
A brilliant blue light, the size of a tiny seed; the subtle abode of the inner Self, and the vehicle by means of which the soul travels from one world to another, either in meditation or at the time of death.

CHAKRA [*cakra*]
(*lit.*, wheel) A centre of energy located in the subtle body where the subtle nerve channels converge like the spokes of a wheel. *See also* KUNDALINI SHAKTI.

CONSCIOUSNESS
The intelligent, supremely independent, divine energy that creates, pervades, and supports the entire universe.

DAKSHINA [*dakṣiṇā*]
An offering or gift to God or the Guru.

DHARANA [*dhāraṇā*]
A centring technique, a spiritual exercise that leads one to the experience of God within.

DIKSHA [*dīkṣā*]
Yogic initiation; the spiritual awakening of a disciple by the grace of the Master. *See also* SHAKTIPAT.

GURU [*guru*]
A spiritual Master who has attained oneness with God and who is able both to initiate seekers and to guide them on the spiritual path to liberation. A Guru is also required to be learned in the scriptures and must belong to a lineage of Masters. *See also* SIDDHA.

GURU GITA [*śrī gurugītā*]
(*lit.*, song of the Guru) A sacred text consisting of *mantras* that describe the nature of the Guru, the Guru-disciple relationship, and techniques of meditation on the Guru. In Siddha Yoga *āśrams*, *Śrī Gurugītā* is chanted every morning.

GURU'S FEET
The scriptures revere the Guru's feet, which are said to embody Shiva and Shakti, knowledge and action, the emission and reabsorption of creation. Powerful vibrations of *śakti* flow from the Guru's feet. They are a mystical source of grace and illumination, and a figurative term for the Guru's teachings.

INNER SOUND
Spontaneous inner sounds (*nāda* in Sanskrit) that may be heard during advanced stages of meditation; *nāda* may take the form of sounds such as bells, the blowing of a conch, and thunder.

KARMA [*karma*]
(*lit.*, action) 1) Any action — physical, verbal or mental. 2) Destiny, which is caused by past actions, mainly those of previous lives.

KUNDALINI SHAKTI
[*kuṇḍalinīśakti*]
The supreme power, the primordial energy that lies coiled at the base of the spine. Through the descent of grace (*śaktipāt*), this extremely subtle force, also described as the supreme Goddess, is awakened and begins to purify the entire being.

MANTRA [*mantra*]
(*lit.*, sacred invocation) Sacred words or divine sounds invested with the power to protect, purify and transform the individual who repeats them. A *mantra* received from an enlightened Master is filled with the power of the Master's attainment.

MAYA [*māyā*]
The term used in the *Vedas* for the power that veils the true nature of the Self and projects the experiences of multiplicity and separation from God.

OM [oṃ]
The primal sound from which the universe emanates; the inner essence of all *mantras*.

RIG VEDA [ṛgveda]
The oldest of the four *Vedas*; it is composed of more than a thousand hymns, including those that invoke the gods of the fire ritual. See also VEDAS.

RUMI, JALAL AL-DIN
(1207-1273) An ecstatic saint of Persia and Turkey who was transformed from a sober scholar into an intoxicated lover of God after one meeting with his Master, Shams-i Tabriz. His poetry is one of the treasures of world literature.

SADHANA [sādhanā]
1) A spiritual discipline or path. 2) Practices, both physical and mental, on the spiritual path.

SAHASRARA [sahasrāra]
The thousand-petalled spiritual energy centre at the crown of the head, where one experiences the highest states of consciousness. See also CHAKRA; KUNDALINI SHAKTI.

SAPTAH [saptāḥ]
A term introduced by Swami Muktananda to refer to the continuous chanting of the name of God, which also may be accompanied by dancing in a circle as an act of devotion and a joyful experience of meditation in motion.

SELF
Divine Consciousness residing in the individual, described as the witness of the mind or the pure I-awareness.

SHAKTI [śakti]
1) The divine Mother; the dynamic aspect of supreme Shiva and the creative force of the universe. 2) Spiritual energy. See also KUNDALINI SHAKTI.

SHAKTIPAT [śaktipāta]
(lit., descent of grace) Yogic initiation in which a Siddha Guru transmits spiritual energy into the seeker, thereby awakening his dormant kuṇḍalinīśakti. See also GURU; KUNDALINI SHAKTI.

SHAMBHAVI MUDRA [śāmbhavīmudrā]
(lit., state of supreme Shiva) A state of spontaneous or effortless meditation, in which the eyes become focused within and the mind delights in the inner Self without any attempt at concentration.

SHIVA [śiva]
1) A name for the one supreme Reality. 2) God as the destroyer, often understood by *yogīs* as the destroyer of barriers to one's identification with the supreme Self.

SHRI [śrī]
1) A term of respect that means sacredness, abundance, beauty, grace and auspiciousness, and signifies mastery of all these. 2) Lakshmi, the goddess of beauty and prosperity.

SHRI SUKTA [śrīsūkta]
A hymn from the Rgveda invoking the goddess Shri.

SIDDHA [siddha]
An enlightened yogi; one who lives in the state of unity-consciousness; one whose experience of the supreme Self is uninterrupted and whose identification with the ego has been dissolved.

SPIRITUAL PRACTICES
Activities, such as meditation, chanting, mantra repetition, selfless service and contemplation that purify and strengthen the mind and body for progress on the spiritual path. See also SADHANA.

TAMASIC
Pertaining to or displaying characteristics of tamas. One of the three basic qualities of nature (gunas), tamas is associated with darkness, dullness and ignorance. The other two gunas are sattva (purity) and rajas (activity).

TAPASYA [tapasyā]
(lit., heat) 1) Austerities. 2) The fire of yoga; the heat generated by spiritual practices.

THIRD EYE
See AJNA CHAKRA.

TURIYA [turīya]
The transcendental state, in which the true nature of reality is directly perceived; the state of deep meditation that lies beyond the waking, dream, and deep-sleep states.

VEDAS [veda]
(lit., knowledge) Among the most ancient, revered and sacred of the world's scriptures, the four Vedas are regarded as divinely revealed, eternal wisdom. They are the Rgveda, Atharvaveda, Sāmaveda, and Yajurveda.

VRITTIS [vrtti]
Fluctuations or movements of the mind; thoughts.

WITNESS
The transcendental Consciousness lying at the root of the mind and from which the mind can be observed. See also CONSCIOUSNESS; SELF.

YOGABHUMI [yogabhūmi]
The land of yoga.

About
Gurumayi Chidvilasananda

About
Gurumayi Chidvilasananda

*S*WAMI CHIDVILASANANDA IS A spiritual teacher in
the ancient yogic tradition. As the head of a lineage of
meditation Masters, she continues the time-honoured
role of sages in every tradition – helping seekers awaken
to their own inner greatness and to the divinity in-
herent in the universe. Gurumayi follows in the foot-
steps of her spiritual Master, Swami Muktananda, who
took the teachings and practices of the path of Siddha
Yoga meditation to the West in the 1970s, in what
he called a "meditation revolution". Before he took
mahāsamādhi in 1982, he selected Gurumayi as his
successor and ordained her as a *saṃnyāsin* in the
Saraswati order. Swami Muktananda Paramahamsa was
himself the successor to Bhagawan Nityananda, a much-
revered saint of modern India.

GURUMAYI CHIDVILASANANDA

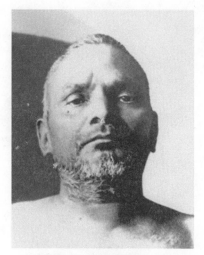

BHAGAWAN NITYANANDA

SWAMI MUKTANANDA

Gurumayi travels widely, taking the teachings and practices of this path to seekers in many countries. She has conducted thousands of programmes in cities around the world, as well as in the two major āśrams of Siddha Yoga meditation: Gurudev Siddha Peeth in Ganeshpuri, Maharashtra, and Shree Muktananda Ashram in South Fallsburg, New York.

The mission of Siddha Yoga meditation is also carried out by a number of trusts established for specific functions. For example, Prasad Chikitsa carries out charitable work in the Tansa Valley, Maharashtra; The Muktabodha Indological Research Institute is dedicated to the study, preservation and dissemination of the ancient scriptural wisdom of India; and Chitshakti Publications is the trust that publishes and distributes the Siddha Yoga meditation books in India.

Wherever Gurumayi travels in the world, whatever form her work takes, her focus remains the same. She calls on people everywhere to wake up to their inner strength and to put into action the natural joy that abounds in their hearts. "The light of the truth is infinite," says Gurumayi, "and this infinite light must definitely be translated into everyday life."

Books by
Gurumayi Chidvilasananda

GEMS FROM THE MAGIC OF THE HEART
In these profound and tender reflections on divine love, selected from a larger volume, Gurumayi makes it clear that the supreme Heart is a place we must get to know. It is here, she tells us, in the interior of the soul, that *"the Lord reveals Himself every second of the day."*

KINDLE MY HEART
"See that whatever happens is a great blessing," Gurumayi says. This is a selection of her talks on the classic themes of the spiritual journey — meditation, *mantra*, control of the senses, the Guru, the disciple and the state of a great being. With clarity, compassion and humour she shows us how to witness the play of the mind and turn it inward towards its source.

INNER TREASURES
"Every heart blazes with divine light," Gurumayi says. *"Every heart trembles with divine love."* In these inspiring talks, she offers us practical ways to cultivate the inner treasures: peace, joy, and love.

THE YOGA OF DISCIPLINE
"From the standpoint of the spiritual path," Gurumayi says, *"the term discipline is alive with the joyful expectancy of divine fulfilment."* In this series of talks on practising and cultivating discipline of the wandering senses, Gurumayi shows us how this practice brings great joy.

MY LORD LOVES A PURE HEART:
THE YOGA OF DIVINE VIRTUES
Fearlessness, reverence, compassion, freedom from anger — Gurumayi describes how these magnificent virtues are an integral part of our true nature. The list of virtues introduced is based on chapter 16 of the *Bhagavadgītā.*

Books by
Swami Muktananda Paramahamsa

PLAY OF CONSCIOUSNESS

CHITSHAKTI VILAS

In this intimate and powerful portrait, Baba Muktananda describes his own journey to Self-realization, revealing the process of transformation he experienced under the guidance of his Guru, Bhagawan Nityananda.

WHERE ARE YOU GOING?

... and what is the purpose of life? Have we lost sight of our true destination? In essays, stories and conversation, Baba offers us an insight into the spiritual quest: how we can embark on it and how it will unfold. This is an essential guidebook for the spiritual journey. *"The heart is the house of God.... Go there,"* he tells us.

BHAGAWAN NITYANANDA OF GANESHPURI

He rarely spoke, but a brief sentence from him spoke volumes, guiding the fortunate listener across the sea of illusion. This volume on Bhagwan Nityananda's life is filled with the observations, thoughts, offerings of praise and heart-warming stories — compiled from many sources over many years — by his greatest disciple and successor, the Siddha Master Swami Muktananda Paramahamsa.

SIX LITTLE BOOKS

The Self is Already Attained — A Book for the Mind — I Love You
I Welcome You All with Love — To Know the Knower — God is with You

Books of aphorisms from Swami Muktananda that are available as a set or individually. Each one is a delight in itself, and each aphorism offers opportunities for sweet, searching comptemplation as it takes us to the heart of the book's subject.

To order these or other books in English, Hindi, Marathi or Gujarati, please write for a current Price List to:

CHITSHAKTI BOOKSTORE,
P.O. GANESHPURI,
DISTRICT THANE,
MS 401 206.